building with harmony: architecture at the service of wholeness

A dramatic expansion in the burgeoning fields of sustainable design, ecological environments, and green building has been gradually replacing conventional building methods. Simultaneously, expertise in more traditional building practices such as feng shui and geomancy (earth energy studies) has also experienced increasing demand, as such knowledge has gradually become standard practice on many building programs and construction projects.

The importance of these traditional techniques resides in their ability to translate a very complex understanding of the interrelationships between the natural world, cosmological forces, the built environment, and human nature into relatively simple terms. Developed as ways with which to maximize human and natural potential, these techniques have direct application to architecture, planning and interior design, as well as management and institutional programming. Through them we can help our clients achieve prosperity, satisfaction, and health.

Contemporary building professionals are concerned with sustainability and ecological accountability. Geomancy and feng shui not only recognize the need for such practices, but they also provide a psychological and spiritual context within which to explore them. Because these methods approach nature directly, they are admirably suited to help us re-establish our relationships to the land, our ancestry as manifested in buildings and landscapes, and to the spiritual forces contained in the earth, natural phenomena, and the biosphere.

I invite you to consider these ideas as you explore some of the projects we have been involved with in which our expertise on geomancy and feng shui played a central role. My hope is that together we will be able to create not only much better buildings, but a richer experience for all.

– Alex Stark

Forest Crossing
Sagaponack, NY

The proprietors of this beautiful home in Sagaponack, NY, designed by the acclaimed firm of Hariri and Hariri, requested full use of feng shui and geomancy techniques in the design and furbishing of their city and country homes. Our contributions included strategies intended to promote health, success, prosperity, and family harmony.

The owners had highly demanding careers. They required a home that could double as a retreat for rest and recuperation as well as a place for social interaction and business meetings. By working in tandem with design professionals, it was possible to create environments that not only reflected the hopes and aspirations of its users, but which were fully conscious of their role in promoting health and harmony. This includes materials, decor, and specifications reflecting green building concerns, electromagnetic safety, and sustainability. In addition, rituals and ceremonies were carried out to promote well-being, encourage success, and to protect its occupants from any unwanted developments.

Residential Environments

Every home is a reflection of the internal aspects of a person's life: it is a holographic projection of its user in which every individual room or space mirrors the entirety of that person's life. The shape of the structure and its internal layout are always reflective of the occupants' personal issues: career, prosperity, health, family dynamics, spirituality, or reputation are all reflected within the home. The entrance, for example, might play an important role in the users' finances or reputation; the kitchen might show how a family relates to each other; dining rooms might show how power is distributed among family members; bedrooms might attest to the love and compassion in a marriage; basements, attics, or closets may reflect the more internal or subconscious aspects in the occupants' lives. The sum of these components can, therefore, provide a useful insight into the goals, aspirations, and dreams held by these individuals, as well as the hard reality of their challenges, obstacles, and fears.

Feng shui analysis of a home consists in a two-fold search for positive factors that can support and enhance the occupants' goals while simultaneously seeking to identify any negative factors that may be impinging on their success. The objective of this analysis is to activate and enhance the positive aspects of the home while also seeking to eliminate or–at the very least–neutralize the negative ones. The result of the feng shui process is a strategy designed to create transformation, improvement, or resolution in the client's life.

Feng shui postulates that all aspects, events, and potential in human life are related and connected to all others. Acknowledging the client's personal goals and aspirations is therefore an integral part of this endeavor; no home can be analyzed independently of its occupants' potential. Furthermore, improvements in one area of the home are bound to have a positive impact in others. It is this holistic outlook on human growth and maturation that allows feng shui to create changes and improvements in areas of life that are resistant to other disciplines.

In addition to the interior of a home, feng shui can also provide specialized techniques for the analysis and development of gardens, landscaping, and exterior features, as well as their corresponding conceptual, material, and symbolic interaction. The synergetic relationship between the outer envelope of the structure and its internal qualities, materials, and colors can be enhanced to promote a healthier, happier, and more prosperous life for all occupants.

425 Park Avenue, Manhattan, NYC

425 Park Avenue is the first skyscraper to be constructed in midtown Manhattan in over 60 years. Designed by the architectural firm of Foster + Partners, this structure is located in an important landmark area that includes such iconic structures as the Chrysler Building, the Empire State Building, the Seagram Building, and Lever House. This extraordinary building was constructed using a slip-in method, in which the new structure is inserted into the old before dismantling the older support system. This was done to prevent structural damage, achieve greater floor heights, and to conform with New York City's requirement for reuse of existing structures.

In addition to complex structural issues, this building posed special feng shui challenges in its unabashed use of glass and metal throughout its entire height as well as the remarkable height of each floor, reaching up to 45 feet in some cases. This required specialized feng shui techniques to prevent energy loss to the outside, and stagnation within taller spaces.

Office Environments

Feng shui and geomancy can create powerful opportunities for the promotion of business and commercial success. This is achieved through a combination of techniques that address the potential of the business site, its architecture and layout, the authority and leadership of its management, and the efficiency and performance of its labor force. These methods can contribute to the fame and recognition of the enterprise, its financial and monetary prowess, and its competitiveness and influence. They can also create synergies between business, community, and the environment.

In order to do this, we look at the configuration of streets and roads leading to the site, the disposition and orientation of the structure, and the flow of vital energy that nourishes the various activities contained therein. We analyze energy flow within the structure and within its component spaces. Offices, work areas, conference rooms, and break rooms are evaluated in order to optimize them for productivity, performance, leadership, and communication. By promoting proper flow and alignment, opportunities are encouraged, potential is maximized, and prosperity is enhanced. In addition, we have specialized techniques for promoting business growth, securing client satisfaction, and increasing staff efficiency.

In addition, special feng shui techniques can be used to evaluate the relative potential of different sectors within a site for specific functions, activities, organizations, or individuals. These can then be correlated with analyses of the patterns of energy flow in the land and buildings in order to determine the most effective configuration for all components of a site. These techniques are extremely helpful when creating new configurations, or adjusting to changes in personnel or footprint.

In situations where business success is compromised, our services can provide cures for diminishing financial returns, institutional vulnerability, compromised reputation, client dissatisfaction, excessive staff turnover, and failing productivity. Specialized techniques can also be used to address situations in which key individuals may be facing competition, vulnerability, or stress. Individual spaces can be tailored to help its user maximize personal and institutional potential.

Our techniques have been successful in creating recognition for client such as Morgan Stanley, Dean Witter, Hyatt Hotels, Whole Foods Markets, Prudential Douglas Elliman, Swarovsky Crystals, Reebok USA, and many others. We have also provided feng shui and geomancy services for such iconic structures as The New York Times Building, the Conde Nast Building, and 425 Park Avenue, featured on this page.

Beekman Hotel
New York, NY

The Beekman is a one of the top luxury hotels in New York City, built in one of its most important historical buildings. Completed in 1883–the same year as the Brooklyn Bridge–the structure holds landmark status in the city of New York as one of its first skyscrapers and one of the more important architectural achievements of that period.

The heart of this building is its nine-story atrium. Capped by a pyramidal skylight, this one-of-a-kind feature has been passionately restored, illuminating the hotel from within. The upper levels are decorated with Victorian wrought-iron railings and bronze balustrades and ornamented with flowers, dragons, and sunbursts. On the main floor, the atrium forms a stage where guests can gather in a series of intimate seating areas.

Our involvement dates to its earliest stages of development, when the original owners approached us to help them secure investors and financing. Over the years, we have been participants in the planning, construction, and launching of this remarkable hotel.

Hospitality

It has been said that success in the hospitality industry is only as good as the last happy customer. This old adage attests to the vulnerability of the industry as a whole and to its dependence on excellence and quality in produce and service. It also attests to the proficiency, perseverance, and flexibility of successful hospitality providers.

The hospitality industry is constantly faced with shifting tastes, trends, and expectations. Reputation is everything, and given the speed of communication afforded by social media, all it takes is a couple of bad reviews to severely compromise the very life of a business. In addition, whether it is a restaurant, hotel, cruises ship, or neighborhood club, the rising cost of real estate and of operations has made investors more important than ever in the decision-making process of many businesses. Firms that once prided themselves on their creative and financial independence have come under the yoke of Wall Street or private investors. Recent research by the New York Times indicates that while hotels and restaurants are providing some of the best food and service ever seen, more businesses are failing due to rising costs, lack of investor commitment, and greater pressure placed by shareholders.

Traditional feng shui techniques can go a long way to optimize the initial space for a restaurant, hotel, or travel venue. However, in the context of hospitality, the need to quickly and constantly change design, effect, and feeling in these spaces means that what might work today will be outmoded tomorrow. Versatility, flexibility, and economy become as important to the feng shui consultant as stability, security, and quality. Hence, our input has to provide multiple alternatives that can be readily adapted for future uses or when changes in fashion or customer expectations demand quick remodeling or improved decor.

Against the backdrop of viral reviews and internet shaming, feng shui techniques that focus on maximizing operational efficiencies can also be combined with procedures designed to protect the reputation and integrity of the operators and suppliers in the long chain of production, management, and distribution proper to this industry. Feng shui also provides specialized rituals to neutralize aggressive tactics and hostile consumers.

Our input has been requested by restaurants of the stature of The Four Seasons (NYC), Fiamma (NYC), DNA (Montreal) and hotels chains such as The Four Seasons, One & Only, Rosewood, and Hyatt.

College of Arts and Design, School of Architecture, Minneapolis, MN

The College of Art and Design is located on the Saint Paul and Minneapolis campuses of the University of Minnesota. It offers instruction in the fields of architecture, graphic design, interior design, landscape architecture, apparel design, product design, and retail merchandising. It includes 23 graduate degree programs as well as nine research centers and a museum of design and arts.

Our input was requested by the faculty of the architecture division in order to expand their understanding of feng shui and geomancy in the context of architectural practice. To this end, we were asked to evaluate their campus and provide a critique of its planning, design, and decor for the benefit of graduate students. This input was then used to make improvements to the existing layout, and to teach students on the application of feng shui and geomancy concepts in their own design programs.

Education and Higher Learning

Of all the areas in which we are involved, education is perhaps the most rewarding. By helping to design and build educational environments, we have been able to contribute to the growth and cultivation of student populations, and to the dissemination of new ideas and models of thinking that include holism, environmental consciousness, and respect for the land and the web of nature.

Educational environments present special challenges to the geomancer because these spaces must serve a complex array of needs. They must provide calm containment of energy for intense, independent focus and, at the same time, include fluid adaptability, interactivity, and communication. Spaces must also be able to symbolically and metaphorically embody the philosophical and aesthetic principles of the institution. They must also provide contact with natural forces in order to sustain intellectual activity, which would be otherwise stunted by lack of physical movement or other types of creative stimuli. This creates special restrictions and conditions for the management of light, ventilation, materials, and views.

We have been involved in a wide range of projects, from early education to institutions of higher learning such as colleges and universities. In all of these cases our fundamental objective has been to improve the educational environment through the use of a more holistic approach to learning. Our contributions include site assessments, evaluations of energy flow, recommendation for interior design, and personalized adjustments for individual classrooms, recreational facilities, and educational offices. We have also participated in focus groups and visioning sessions, and have helped develop guidelines for improved materials, lighting and decor. In addition, we have also produced instructional booklets highlighting the fundamental role of energy, imagery, and symbolism in the classroom.

Among other contributions, we have assisted the Board of Education of the City of New York in the creation of improved classrooms and management offices. We have also collaborated with specialized learning facilities such as the Center for Discovery, a facility that serves intellectually challenged children and teenagers, and with Skyshapers, a motivational program for early teens. We helped design and provided construction rituals for the Waterside School, a remarkable preparatory high-school for disadvantaged kids located in Stamford, CT and instructed graduate students on feng shui and geomancy at the Department of Architecture, University of California Berkeley, and at the University of Minnesota's School of Architecture.

Weisman Art Museum
Minneapolis, MN

Founded in 1943 as part of the University of Minnesota, this museums houses a collection of over 30,000 objects including works by Biederman, Maurer, and Hartley, and a large collection of Mimbres Pottery and Korean furniture. The building was designed by architect Frank Ghery, and is considered seminal in his development as an architect.

We were invited by the staff of the museum to make an evaluation of its performance, and to suggest improvements to the flow and efficiency of its layout. Changing needs had demanded improved traffic flow, visitor comfort, and additional educational spaces. In addition, this was also an opportunity to expand our educational outreach to architectural practitioners and students interested in incorporating feng shui and geomancy into their work.

The Arts

Artistic expression is of the greatest importance to all persons regardless of nationality or culture. The arts transcend all boundaries and serve as a common language for all peoples. It is one of the few arenas in which everybody can participate and which can also elevate and cultivate individuals of all ages. Within individual cultures, the arts also represent the expression of that culture's deepest feelings which, in their most exalted manifestations, can reach spiritual and intellectual heights. Hence, the development, cultivation, and dissemination of artworks, music, dance, poetry, and other forms of expression is and should be a priority of all nations. This goes in tandem with education and policy, as it is important for school systems and governments to partake in the arts as a way to promote a well-educated and cosmopolitan population.

The arts in the US operate at a distinct disadvantage when compared with European and Asian counterparts. Other governments will often finance artistic output lavishly and use it as part of their national or regional image-making. In the US, it most often falls on philanthropies and private donors to bridge weak or lacking government funding. Often these institutions run deficits when trying to combine exhibition and performance buildings with extensive outdoor and entertainment areas, hosting visitors and participants in large numbers, and requiring expensive staffing and maintenance. In the private arts market, it is not uncommon for arts entrepreneurs to invest large sums of money on plays, performances, or artworks to see their artists outmaneuvered by foreign dealers and discount brands. Furthermore, increasing competition and the advent of internet sales have eroded already thin profit margins. Keeping on top of these changing trends while maintaining profits and exposure can be exhausting to both capital and personnel.

Despite these shortcomings, feng shui can be used to great advantage in museums, galleries, and performance halls, as its contributions extend beyond the stage or exhibition space and into offices, meeting rooms, and decision-making areas. Our participation in these spaces has been complex. While endeavoring to optimize the arts space for interactions with the audience and public, behind the scenes we have also strived to enhance the organization's recognition, public exposure, influence, and income potential. In many cases, it was also important to neutralize extreme competition, weak appreciation, and negative press.

**Doerr-Hosier Center,
Aspen Institute,
Aspen, Colorado**

The Doerr-Hosier Center at the Aspen Institute provides administrative and conferencing space for this prestigious think tank, which attracts heads of state, researchers, and scholars from around the world. Completed in 2007, the LEED-certified structure is perhaps best defined by its interdependence with the landscape and nature of Aspen and as a method of inspiring and facilitating communication. The site includes a magnificent meadow, meandering creeks, superb views, and groves of Aspens. This was also be the last structure to be built in this historically important campus, which includes buildings by Fritz Benedict and Herbert Bayer.

Feng shui criteria was used to evaluate the site and to propose optimal location, orientation, and alignments for the new facility. The project was conceived with full geomantic consideration, including alignments to significant mountains as well as rituals to promote prosperity, success and health.

Government & NGOs

We are living at a time in history when traditional governmental structures are slowly loosing power and influence to non-governmental organizations (NGOs), community institutions, and internet peer groups. This has created both a challenge and an opportunity, as the various concerns of the citizenry adjust to new modalities better suited to put forth their demands and programs. At the same time, traditional organizations must find ways to adapt to these changes, creating more flexible patterns of management and communication, and better strategies for implementation.

Feng shui and geomancy encompass many techniques used to elevate the political and governance potential of an organization. When used with a high level of sophistication, these techniques and methods can help to enhance the power, reach, and influence of institutions at the regional, national or international levels. Geomancy, in particular, is an effective tool that can help to make institutions, NGOs, and governmental organizations into more effective, influential and responsible bodies.

To achieve this requires an understanding of the impacts of land form, orientation, and location on the performance of a structure. These, in turn, can shed light on the site's potential to generate power, responsibility, and influence. They include assessments of land and water patterns, road and traffic influences, and the flow of vital energy throughout the site and its buildings. The latter include evaluations of earth forces, geomagnetic influences, and geopathic stresses (harmful underground energies). In addition, other techniques can evaluate the relative potential of the site at specific moments in time. Using these approaches, for example, it is possible to determine the likelihood of success or failure for issues concerning wealth, political influence, or intellectual reach at specific locations within a site, and at different points in time.

In addition, special feng shui techniques can be used to evaluate the relative potential of different sectors of a site for specific functions, activities, organizations, or individuals. These can then be correlated with analyses of the patterns of energy flow in the land and buildings in order to determine the most effective configuration for all components of a site.

We have had the great honor to support agencies within the US government, the United Nations, as well as think tanks (see highlight at left) and NGO's dedicated to creating change in health care, land management, sustainability, and earth sciences.

Intensive Care Unit
Bellevue Hospital, NYC

This state-of-the-art facility represents the consolidation of all intensive care units at Bellevue Hospital, the premier trauma center for the city of New York. Based on an intensivisit medical model, this unit brings together all units previously under departmental control into one space, which occupies a complete floor in this large medical complex.

Our contribution consisted in assessments of the holistic qualities of space in relation to state-of-the-art technology. By manipulating the internal environment, we sought ways to cue the patient to the rhythms of nature through a variety of approaches: fluctuations of light and sound, use of horizon lines, and by opening views along windows that overlook the East River. This project included water fountains whose emanating sound can reach sterile units (photo above). Through these devices we also hoped to reduce ICU dementia, a condition caused in part by the sterility and monotony of the ICU environment.

Health Care Facilities

Our firm has been deeply involved in the health care field, helping to create hospitals, healing centers, and medical spas. Our efforts are based on a keen desire to transform the quality of health care and its delivery toward a more holistic model that is conscious of the role played by the environment in the healing process. This concern is anchored in the curative space, but also extends to the patient's home, which we see as an extension of the human body, and therefore, capable of promoting health as well as disease. From the perspective of feng shui and geomancy, health and healing are the result of harmony and balance in all areas of human life, including the spaces in which we live and work.

In the context of healthcare, this includes the type of construction in the hospital or clinic space, its energetic qualities, its history, as well as the kind of thoughts and emotions these spaces are capable of eliciting in us when we are subjected to procedures and cures, often of an invasive nature. In the modern context, this also has to include how much technological, chemical, or visual pollution we are subjected to, as well as the institutional and medical interventions required by each medical modality. Managing these often competing considerations can be daunting, particularly when the health of the individual is pressing and medical and regulatory protocols are in place.

The creation of a health care facility requires both technological and spiritual approaches. Through the use of holistic techniques, which combine traditional feng shui, healing rituals, and green building techniques, we have sought to contribute to the creation of vibrant spaces, fully capable of promoting health and recuperation. In addition, we have also tried to educate health care personnel in the performance of energy clearing processes and maintenance rituals.

Our work in this field includes collaborations with Beth Israel Hospital (NY), Continuum Health Partners (NY), Bellevue Hospital (NY), Sutter Health Partners (CA), St. Mary's Duluth Medical Center (MN), Denver Cardiology Associates (CO) as well as smaller clinics and private practices. In all of these cases we provided feng shui and geomancy input for architects, designers, and health care professionals concerning techniques used to develop a greater understanding of the role of nature, the land, and the energetic environment on the healing process. We have also lectured extensively, promoting not only the vision of holistic healing, but also advocating for a paradigm shift towards greater prevention and sustainability.

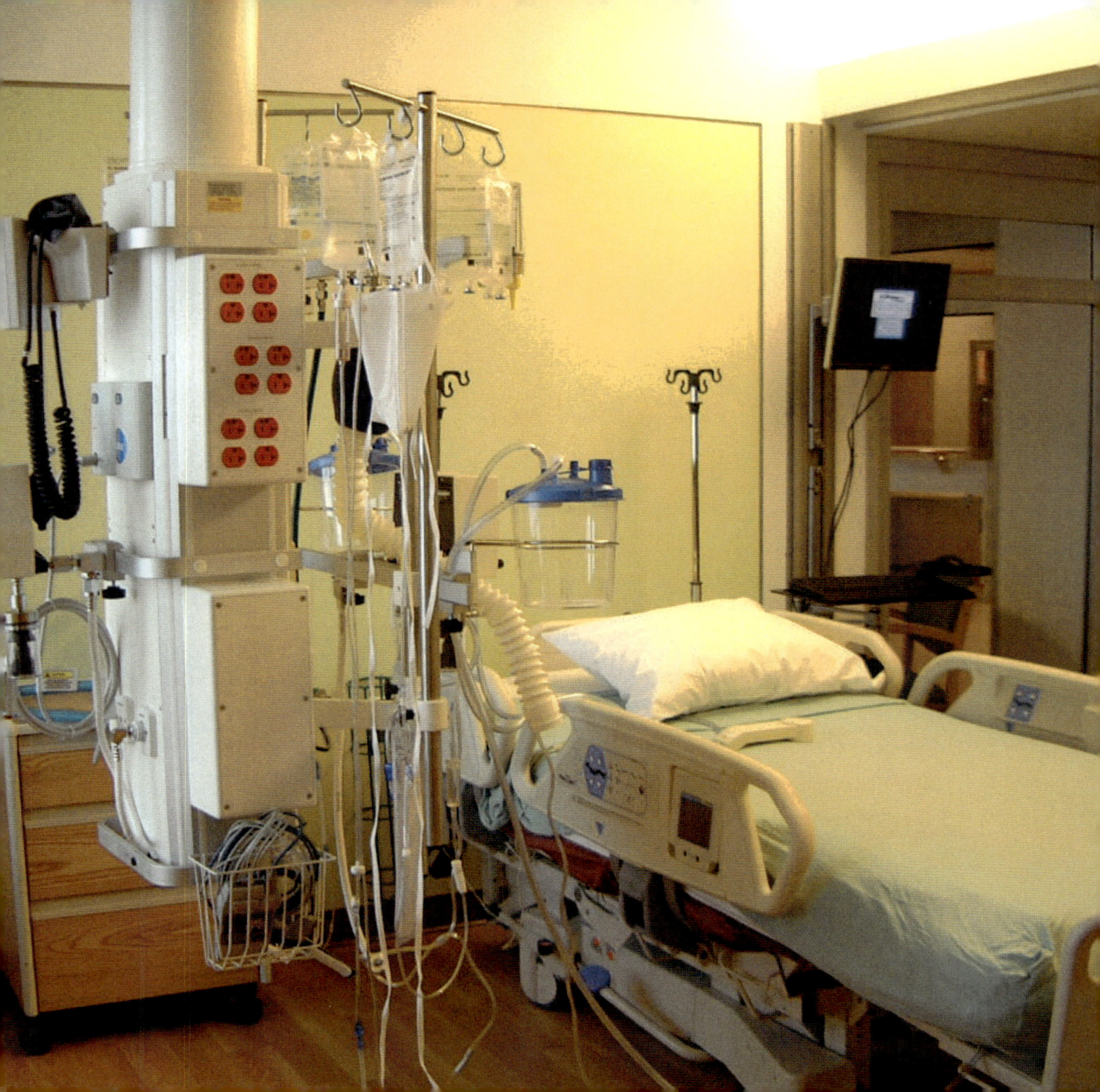

Reebok International Ltd.
Boston MA

Reebok International Limited is an American footwear and apparel company and a subsidiary of German sporting goods giant Adidas. Reebok produces and distributes fitness, running and CrossFit sportswear, including clothing and footwear. The Reebok brand also includes over 20,000 training studios in eight countries and is a major sponsor of international sports.

Our participation was focused on their new headquarters in Boston, which now enfolds their flagship store (pictured above and at right), an experimental CrossFit gym, and other sport training facilities. It also includes creative and design operations, testing labs, and training and education programs. Optimizing sales and increasing the brand's recognition and status were central to our task, at a time when online sales and heavy competition have made inroads into traditional brick and mortar stores. In this we were supported by their space planning team, architectural and interiors professionals, and fashion consultants.

Retail & Sales

Retail and sales present exciting opportunities for the application of feng shui and geomancy. Not only is it necessary in these cases to promote the prerequisite prosperity, recognition, and success, but this has to be done against the background of changing trends, fashions, idiosyncrasies, and the increasingly instable vagaries of the marketplace. Exploding use of internet tools for purchasing have significantly eroded the primacy of brick and mortar stores, with increasingly worrisome indicators for established malls and shopping centers. As a consequence, the retail sector is undergoing rapid transformation as traditional shopping patterns give way to quicker transactions, more attention being paid to influencers and internet presence, and to a greater need to satisfy individual requirements and expectations.

Against this backdrop, our objective has been to increase sales, expand market share, and add to the recognition of the brand or product while simultaneously attempting to neutralize the negative effects of rapid change. Increasingly, our efforts have also focused on the creation of transformational experiences for shoppers and staff. Customers are demanding that products perform not only as functional objects but also as part of the their personal journey of discovery. From the design of the product to its manufacture and display, sales efforts now present a coordinated effort that is aware of the economic, psychological, and spiritual needs of the producer, the consumer, and the sales staff.

Part of this trend has focused on the need to enhance a business's edge against increasingly competitive markets. In addition, a new market consciousness now pays a great deal of attention to the inter-relationships between consumer and ethics, between dollar spent and its impact on the biosphere, and to the communal imperative for sustainability. Staff recruitment, development, and satisfaction are also part of this trend. These, as well as the more traditional concerns for profitability, recognition and success, are part and parcel of the needs our services can address.

Despite this unpredictability, our techniques are very well suited to this area of business, and we have successfully advised sales establishments of all types and sizes, from boutique shops, to regional realty concerns, national chains, and multinational traders. Clients include Reebok, Swarovski, David Yurman, Garfield & Marks, Zulily, Whole Foods Markets, and Urban Outfitters.

THE

Swarovsksy Crystals
Wattens, Ausria

Currently run by the fifth generation of family members, Swarovski is an Austrian producer of glass and g;ass products headquartered in Wattens, Austria.

This large conglomerate is split into three major industry areas: Swarovski Crystal Business primarily produces lead glass, jewelry and accessories; Swarovski Optik produces binoculars, telescopes, and telescopic sights for rifles; and Tyrolit, a manufacturer of grinding, sawing, drilling, and dressing tools, as well as a supplier of tools and machines. Swarovski has a global reach of approximately 3,000 stores in around 170 countries, more than 29,000 employees, and a revenue of about 2.7 billion euros. All Swarovski crystal produced since 2012 have been lead-free.

Our input for this client consisted in optimization of their headquarters offices in Wattens (Austria), New York City, and London, as well as input on manufacturing processes and retail outlets.

Industry & Manufacturing

Industry presents special challenges to the feng shui consultant. On one hand there is the need to promote prosperity and to create value from business activity. On the other hand, there is a need to minimize industry's impact on the earth and the biological web. In fact, many of our clients are actively involved in creating new paradigms in which industry itself becomes an agent of healing and regeneration.

Whether it is a wine manufacturer, a metals producer, or a printing plant, our clients have sought our advice in order to create environments that are efficient, productive, supportive of staff and management, and as green and sustainable as possible. In addition, many of them are also exploring the possibility of working with new systems and technologies that allow for more ecologically conscious use of resources, energy, and time.

Traditional feng shui considerations can greatly enhance an industry's prospects for financial rewards, staff and client satisfaction, good management, and conscious business practices. Worker productivity, communication, and management are other areas in which specialized geomantic techniques can be of help. In addition, certain rituals are very effective at promoting success and minimizing risks. Accidents, overages, inefficiency, and waste are some of the many concerns that can be minimized through the use of these techniques.

Furthermore, the global reach of transnational industries can also be enhanced through judicious management of energies internal to the business structure as well as by assessments and adjustments to the environment of both factory space and corporate headquarters. In an increasingly global market, maintaining a competitive edge and anticipating changes in production, distribution, retail, and customer trends has become an overriding concern of all industrial efforts. Feng shui and geomancy can provide advantages in all of these areas.

We have used these techniques to support clients such as Swarovsky, an Austrian-based manufacturer of optical glass for military applications as well as the more popular jewelry and fashion accessories; Gerald Metals, a global producer and distributor of metals; Madero Wines, the largest producer of wines and liquors in Mexico; Reebok, the ubiquitous designer and manufacturer of sport equipment and fashions; David Yurman, a designer and manufacturer of luxury jewelry; and Fortuny, a renowned producer of luxury textiles and home accessories based in Italy.

"THE POWER OF EMOTIONS"

Port Imperial
Weehawken, NJ

Port Imperial is a $1.7 billion master planned community on the Hudson River facing midtown Manhattan. It includes over 6,500 residential units, approximately two million square feet of commercial space, and a full service hotel. It is connected to Manhattan by New York Waterway ferries as well as the Hudson–Bergen Light Rail system. Because of this sophisticated transportation network, Port Imperial has become a preferred residential location for city workers and their families.

We were invited by Mack-Cali, the developers, to provide a site analysis of the entire complex as well as to evaluate the design of each building within the campus. Apartment units, common areas, amenities, and outdoor spaces were also evaluated for their suitability as family homes, as places for professional advancement, and as locations for healthy children and families. This complex is in continuous development, with several more building currently in planning.

Real Estate Development

Real estate is a complicated business. Whether it is for housing, offices, retail, hospitality, or mixed uses, developers are constantly pressured by competing interests. They must maximize return on their investors' money while also conforming to stringent code requirements, regulatory guidelines, political imperatives, and public opinion. Often cast as the villains in editorials and in the public imagination, developers must show perseverance and tenacity, as most real estate projects take years if not decades to complete.

Each project has its own identity and its own set of problems. A skyscraper in Manhattan is a completely different undertaking than a mall in California. Condos in New Jersey are not the same as condos in Colorado. Yet in all cases, the imperatives are the same–produce a profit, please the customer, build on schedule and within the budget, and stay away from litigation. Feng shui tools are well suited for this kind of complex scenario. Some techniques are helpful in terms of maximizing profits and return on investment. Others can help achieve auspicious layouts that enhance customer experience, satisfaction, and loyalty. Yet others can be used to avert litigation and regulatory intrusion. Others can help keep construction on schedule and without incidents. These techniques include traditional feng shui analyses of form, location, alignment, and layout, along with rituals to promote successful outcomes, remediate damaged land, or enhance community support and participation. Feng shui can also be used to bolster the developer's output and productivity through interventions at their corporate offices, satellite offices, or showrooms. Feng shui can also help conscious development by promoting sustainability and ecological integrity as well as by connecting the built environment (buildings, gardens) with Nature and the local community.

We have been fortunate to work with creative developers on incredibly diverse projects in the United States and overseas. These include *Port Imperial*, a $1.7 billion master-planed residential community in New Jersey (see highlight at left); *Hilltop*, a 50-acre mixed use complex in the grounds of an old mall in Richmond CA; *Highland Lake*, a rural housing and resort community in Asheville, NC; *Jack London Square*, a multi-use commercial development and community attraction in Oakland CA; *One Brooklyn Bridge Park*, a 1,000,000 square-foot housing structure in New York City; *425 Park Avenue*, the most recent skyscraper to be built on mid-town Manhattan; *Mandarina*, a housing and resort complex in Mexico; and *Wadi Ram*, an eco-housing development in the Kingdom of Jordan.

Highland Lake Development
Hendersonville, NC

The developer of this complex community near Asheville, NC wanted to create a traditional setting that would provide ease of access to residential, commercial, cultural, and agricultural amenities. Focused around a lake with fully developed recreational facilities, this traditional community includes town houses, detached homes, mixed-use commercial development, a lodge and restaurant, an organic farm, a retreat center, and a conservation area with pristine wetlands, all within walking distance from each other. This combination of uses has created a synergy between its various components that respects both the agricultural history and traditions of the area while providing modern development possibilities for a rapidly expanding population.

Our input included a full analysis of the entire complex with a view to improve the site's capture of energy and vitality. The purpose of this assessment was to secure additional investment, enhance brand recognition for the development as a whole, and expand sales of home plots.

Urbanism & Site Planning

Nothing exemplifies classical feng shui knowledge more than large-scale site planning. Though most lay people understand feng shui as a discreet practice to be used in interiors or single buildings, the origins of feng shui–and geomancy in general–are based in observations of large scale terrain (mountain ranges, valleys, entire watersheds) and its interaction with seasons, astrological influences, and weather. Over time, these considerations were narrowed down to include the planning and layout of cities and villages and their relationship to ideal topographical configurations. Only later was this adapted to individual buildings or building sites.

At its root, feng shui is deeply interested in the interplay between a particular location and its larger geographical and geological context. We first assess the quality of the land and its topography in order to determine the relative potential of the area. Geological and geopathic stresses (earth energies detrimental to life) are also diagnosed, as these can pose significant risks to both health and fortune. Recommendations are then made for ideal land use patterns which respect both town planning concerns as well as cosmic and spiritual forces. Ideal location of functions and optimal building orientations are also proposed. Finally, suggestions are made to maximize opportunity and to minimize drawbacks due to poor land massing, improper water patterns, or insufficient earth energy. In addition, guidelines are provided for optimal design of street patterns, service facilities, civic institutions, individual buildings, gardens, and landscaping.

At the same time, feng shui is also interested in contemporary thinking on site planning and urbanism, with particular emphasis on the New Urbanism movement. This movement, which has rapidly influenced urban design across the country, has created a whole new way of looking at land development. Predicated on a more sustainable relationship between buildings and human activity, it shares our concern for a more ecologically and socially conscious approach to urbanization, and for a closer relationship between nature, technology, and the urban fabric.

We have been requested to contribute geomantic recommendations in a variety of land development projects, including residential subdivisions, mixed use neighborhoods, resort developments, and intentional communities. Our contributions have included analyzes of the land patterns in the towns of Desert Hot Springs (CA), Weehawken (NJ), Aspen (CO), Oakland (CA), Rockford (IL), Mill Valley (CA), Hendersonville (NC), Valle de Bravo (Mexico), Chala (Mexico) and Wadi Ram (Kingdom of Jordan).

L/W
MODEL HOMES
COTTAGES (LODGING)
LODGE
SPA
RESTAURANT
STURE
HLICC
CHP
ORGANIC GARDEN
TSH
GH

Mandarina Resort, Riviera Nayarit, Mexico

Located on a pristine beach on the Riviera Nayarit, north of Puerto Vallarta, this luxury resort development will include a collection of private residences, hotels by One & Only and Rosewood, an array of culinary offerings, sports fields, a beach club, and a spa.

More importantly, this development will provide ecological security to an area threatened by development and which includes nesting beaches for marine turtles, protected habitat for jaguars and eagles, and a migratory route for whales and other marine mammals. The development covers over 1,400 acres and includes an entire estuary and adjacent agricultural fields.

We were invited by the local developers to help create a sanctuary space where the spiritual and cultural qualities of this terrain could be protected and which would welcome visitors from abroad while also providing employment to the local population. We collaborated with local healers and shamans on ways to honor and protect the spiritual and energetic qualities of this magnificent land.

Resort Development

Resort development presents contradictory challenges. Typically, the land involved was selected for its natural beauty, integrity, and charm as this is the driver behind visitor satisfaction and sales. On the other hand, resort developments are also part of a region's or nation's global development plans and involve intrusive investment in infrastructure and services. These two concerns–ecological integrity and development needs–tend to collide and contradict each other, with the result that many resort developments end up damaging the very fabric of the landscapes and terrain that made them interesting in the first place. Overdevelopment in Cancun, coral destruction in Thailand and the Philippines, and water depletion in Bali–to mention only a few–have undercut the appeal of these magnificent places, transforming lush, magical landscapes into generic beach developments for mass tourism.

From the feng shui perspective, this amounts to a crime, as it is almost impossible to recover from bad development of this type. Overuse of beach front, intrusion into ecosystems, reduction of habitat, and depletion of resources have marked effects not only on the natural integrity of these locales, but also on their economic feasibility over time. Quick profits are often gained at the expense of future potential. To make matters worse, the local population is often not consulted when making these decisions, which are, more often than not, controlled by overseas financial and banking centers.

Working within this context is nevertheless exciting because, when done right, resorts can also help to forestall other types of development that could be even more intrusive. In recent years, public pressure has forced major resort developers to consider sustainability and ecological integrity as part of their operating processes. National and regional governments have also stepped up their regulatory powers in conjunction with NGOs and academic institutions. After many years of lobbying for participation, native peoples are now being consulted in order to respect and honor their traditions and culture as well as to identify areas that may be sensitive in terms of their history, ancestry, and rituals.

We have been fortunate to participate in this type of development across the United States, in Mexico, Costa Rica, and the Kingdom of Jordan. In all cases we have collaborated with talented architects and planners, in conjunction with local authorities, environmental councils, shamans, and community leaders. In several of these cases, it was possible to change development goals that once included damaging golf and marina construction into ecologically sound development with minimal footprints, protection of endangered species, and inclusion of local participation in the decision-making process.

Ecological Restoration

It is axiomatic that human use of the land will tend to deplete it. Whether it is for agriculture, housing, industry, or commerce, human activity tends to introduce technology, mechanical processes, and removal of top soil and vegetation. This is considered normal in any building campaign, but the impact of this activity tends to invariably degrade the quality of energy in the land, reduce habitat, and deplete natural resources. As soil quality degrades, it is less and less able to support the very uses that brought humans to that particular location. This is a paradox that all civilizations have had to confront, not always with success. There are many examples of entire cultures perishing because of overuse of natural resources, depletion of available water, and degradation of crops. After years of overuse, all it takes is a few years of drought or pests to decimate the land.

Restoring land to its optimal potential is an arduous task, which can take many years. The energy and value depleted by human uses cannot be restored easily or quickly. Land trampled by construction and roads tends to loose its ability to support life. Use of chemical pesticides and fertilizers to boost production may work for a while, but these lead invariably to greater resistance in the genetic makeup of plants and fungi essential to life. Restoration of damaged land must, therefore, combine holistic approaches addressing the chemical toxicity of the land with organic and bio-dynamic approaches to its restoration.

Energy patterns of the land must also be enhanced. These can include dragon veins, ley lines, and energy vortices. These are all energetic components of the land that create the matrices and patterns of energy in healthy soil. Often, these components can be traumatized by industry, agriculture, husbandry, or construction. The resulting negative patterns in the land and in water, known as geopathic stresses or geostress, can wreak havoc and interfere with crops, work activities, and health. As land development and the mechanization of agriculture and industry continue to grow, geostress is becoming ubiquitous, with fewer and fewer locations free of its impact.

Geomancers use specialized techniques to heal geostress. This is tedious work, as it requires repeated interventions over many years and across large areas of terrain. Some of the techniques we use come from feng shui, but many others have been developed by European and Native American geomancers. We strive to combine these techniques in ways that are more effective, and which will work more permanently in all types of land. Geostress remediation is a burgeoning field, with new approaches and techniques being experimented across the globe.

The Center for Discovery, Harris, NY

The Center for Discovery is a pediatric medical facility located in Sullivan County, NY. Based on a holistic model, this 500 acre facility includes a hospital, residences and classrooms for children with multiple frailties, a bio-dynamic farm with its own bakery and guesthouse, a therapeutic equine stable, a dairy farm, a conference center, and areas of unspoiled wilderness. The Center has attracted international attention and is one of the most important pediatric centers for this type of population in the world, with fellowships being offered to students from around the globe.

The Center invited us to assist in the site planning of this extensive campus at a time in its development when the ecological challenges of previous uses–farming, cattle, and slaughtering houses–were becoming more and more apparent (see photo above). They wanted us to focus on remediation of damaged land and on development of healthy building sites. The photo at right shows the same site 7 years later, after geostress healing was completed.

Whole Foods Markets
USA, Canada, and the UK

Whole Food Markets is the fastest growing chain of specialty food markets in the country with shops across the US, Canada, and the UK. Based on a holistic model, Whole Foods Markets offers a combination of organic and conventional produce, health and beauty products, prepared foods, home decor, and body care items.

Created as a way to bring healthy eating to a wider population, each shop is conceived both regionally as well as locally, and local produce and products are included in every store. In addition, the business model is based on a recognition of the critical role played by staff and suppliers as part of the overall sales effort. Whole Foods Market was purchased by Amazon in 2017, and efforts have been made to expand delivery services as well as automation.

Feng shui services have included all phases of design and construction for new stores, from site selection, to early design concepts, to floor layout, materials specifications, and interior design. We have also included site blessings and space clearing rituals as part of our general offerings.

Food & Nutrition

Healthy food and good nutrition are foundations for wellness. Without healthy diets, it becomes difficult to flourish, and this can impact negatively on physical and mental health, work performance, productivity, and education. Research confirms that a proper meal is a greater indicator of school performance than IQ or previous education. Adequate nutrition should be an important priority for all citizens.

Despite this self-evident truth, the fact is that most persons in the US lack in basic nutrition, consuming instead large doses of sugar, salt, fats, and processed foods laced with chemicals and preservatives. This has led to an epidemic of obesity and to increasing mortality and morbidity rates across most segments of the population. The US now ranks lowest among industrialized nations for infant mortality and longevity.

Feng shui is deeply concerned about food, not only in terms of its consumption, but also its production, packaging, and transportation. The quality in food (its *chi*) is directly proportional to the quality of the soils on which it was grown, the manner of handling, integrity of packaging, and time taken for it to reach the consumer. The more direct this transaction, the higher the *chi* content in food. Ideally, consumers would eat directly from the farm, but improving soil quality and reducing transport times are important components of a healthy nutritional approach, even when shopping in super markets.

Healthy soil, in turn, depends on clean water, proper crop rotation, natural fertilization, and safe pollination by bees and other insects. Depletion of water resources has added to this problem by adding greater salinity to soils through pumping of mineralized aquifer waters on agricultural fields. Industrial production of crops, cattle, and fisheries has also increased waste products, including manure and methane, a greenhouse gas responsible for increased climate change. To make matters even more complicated, efforts to improve crop production through organic and bio-dynamic techniques have flooded the market with industrial products, which, though organic, are nevertheless culpable of all the other factors leading to soil depletion mentioned above.

We have been active at a number of levels in efforts to improve soil and nutritional quality as well as on the marketing and sales of food products. From farm production to large grocery chains (see highlight at left), our concern has been on helping producers maximize output and sales while fostering healthy soil and sustainable crops.

Agriculture & Farming

Casa Madero Winery
Monterrey, Mexico

Founded in 1597, Casa Madero is the oldest winery in the Americas. Grapes brought from Spain were mixed with native grapes to produce a disease-resistant variety still in production over 400 years later. Today Casa Madero is the largest producer of wines in Mexico and increasingly important as an exporter of quality organic wines to the European and American market.

The winery consists of 2,000 acres of grape production in the Valle de San Lorenzo and a production facility, which includes a visitors center, tasting rooms, and a full-service hotel for overseas tourism.

Our input included a full analysis of the existing fields and production center in preparation for a full renovation of the visitors center and production buildings. The main challenge was to help Casa Madero position itself as a competitor to better-known brands in the international market. Retaining the original feeling and substance of the early years of Mexican history was an integral component of our task.

Agriculture represents the foundation of civilization: it is impossible to conceive of life without food production. Farms employ over 30 percent of all workers, and account for over 40 percent of all land use. Nevertheless, they are quickly loosing their position in the global economy. In 2018, they only accounted for 3 percent of the world's GDP, down from 4 percent in 2010. This has to do in part with the mechanization of farming processes but also to technological and genetic innovations that have made food production much more efficient than in the past.

These innovations have come with a hidden cost. Use of pesticides, genetic engineering, and chemical treatment of soils has degraded the quality of soil used in agriculture. Depletion of water resources such as aquifers and a deepening crisis in terms of river flow and glacial melting that nourish crops also contribute to a pattern of increasing insecurity in food production. Once productive lands are now becoming fallow in many areas around the globe, as mineral deposits accumulate on soil, water becomes scarce, and crops develop resistance to pest controls.

Traditional feng shui techniques can do little to restore this type of damage to the land, as this is in the domain of soil engineering and regulatory oversight. However, feng shui has much to offer in terms of elevating our respect for the land, and of honoring its sustenance. Many clients come to us in an effort to complement their technical teams with a wider knowledge about the role of land in our common history, and the approaches used to regain some of that traditional respect. Bringing land uses back into harmony with nature is an important task all of humanity will have to undertake if we are to move into a post-chemical world. Feng shui also acknowledges the importance of ancestry in land management and postulates that the energy of our history is contained in the land. Hence, it makes sense to honor it and to treat it with greater respect, not only as a resource for food production, but also as the matrix (Mother) from which all of abundance springs.

Clients in this field have included wineries in Sonoma, the largest wine producer in Mexico (see highlight at left), horse-breeding stables in Canada and the US, as well as family farms and orchards across the country.

Retreat Garden, Valle de Bravo, Mexico

This beautiful garden is a private retreat for a family with roots in the area going back to colonial times. Conceived as a landscape with a healing narrative, the visitor must walk through various levels of terrain, encountering diverse symbolic and metaphorical spaces that include meditation and reflection buildings, art installations, interactive walkways, and chapels naturally constructed out of the existing vegetation.

The garden culminates in a labyrinth based on early medieval models. Its purpose is to guide the visitor into a state of union with the land and with the spiritual qualities present in it in order to re-establish harmony with Nature and with Self.

Our input consisted in an evaluation of the land in terms of its sacred and healing qualities, procedures and rituals to help enhance its positive qualities, and design guidelines to help restore its original beauty and power. We worked closely with landscape designers, permaculture experts, and local gardeners.

Gardens & Landscaping

Gardens and landscaping have the power to connect us to larger cosmic forces and make these available for our delight, regeneration, and healing. By connecting directly with the forces of nature, the seasons, and weather, our senses are stimulated, and our appreciation for beauty is enhanced. In addition, healing power can be harnessed, and connections can be made to our ancestry, our spirituality, and our history. Whether it is in a large conservation area, a healing garden, or in a tiny urban plot, the placement of water, vegetation, rocks, and sculptures can be understood as an exercise in global harmony; each outdoor space, no matter how small, can be a representation of the larger Cosmos.

All of nature can be understood as a repository for the sacred, so in a sense all gardens are healing places. Labyrinths, groves, meadows, sculpture, and outdoor pavilions can all be used to enhance the spiritual power of the land. In all cases landscaping should be seen organically; the seasons should be respected and can be used for their symbolic and regenerative power; the land should be allowed to inform us and direct our efforts. Earth and Sky, the primordial Mother and Father, can serve as guideposts for our own journey through life. Vegetation and the animals it nourishes can be understood as our brothers and sisters in life.

From the perspective of geomancy and feng shui, gardens are a category separate from buildings. Many of the more commonly known feng shui principles and tools commonly used for interiors cannot be used in natural environments; these require approaches of an earlier origin, and depend more deeply on the land's relationship to the sky and to astronomical forces. Whereas the interior of a structure is conceived in terms of the movement of vital energy (chi) and the disposition of objects in space, outdoor environments are more directly correlated to much larger Cosmic forces. Hence, the theoretical constructs and practical tools used for landscaping are substantially different from those used indoors. In addition, landscaping considerations need to be correlated against other factors such as geopathic stresses, the global geomagnetic grids, underground water, and mineral deposits. Furthermore, when working on gardens, we always try to introduce the shamanic knowledge proper to the area as a way to connect more deeply with the land itself, and with the cultural and historical depth provided by the original inhabitants of that land.

Rancho La Puerta
Tecate. Mexico

Rancho La Puerta is one of the oldest and most revered spas in the country. The Ranch–as it is affectionately known–has spawned an entire industry and pioneered almost all the trends that have made American spas known around the world.

Located in the slopes of a sacred mountain, this spa has been renowned for the quality of its water, air, and vegetation. This has allowed it to pioneer fitness and nutritional approaches that are today ubiquitous: fasting, juicing, herbal wraps, hatha yoga, cross-training, sun healing, forest bathing, hot stone massage, and many others. Endowed with extensive trails, The Ranch also pioneered walking meditation as a form of physical and spiritual therapy.

We were invited to help improve on the quality of landscaped areas, on the design of new villas, and on the overall feeling and appeal of the extensive campus. We also performed extensive rituals to honor the land and to promote its health and abundance.

Spas and Retreat Centers

The vertiginous rise of spas and retreat centers over the last decades has reflected a changing consciousness about lifestyles, nutrition, wellness, aging, and the relationships between work and leisure. Spas, in particular, have taken on more complex characteristics, enfolding within their programs and offerings a wide array of alternative modes of therapy, education, and healing. Based on the idea that humans are both body and spirit, spas have been experimenting with alternative modalities that can nourish the physical, emotional, intellectual, and spiritual components of the self.

Retreat centers, on the other hand, have had to adjust to an ever widening demand for education and information about the self and its relationships to nature, family, and the world of spirit. What began as an alternative consciousness in the 1960's and 70's has become part of the mainstream; often these organizations have had to adjust to the consumer market, and now offer learning programs on everything from classical meditation to business planning, lifestyle management, and substance abuse counseling. Rural retreat centers also have to account for their relationship to land, often extensive in scope. In such cases our analyses become as much about the facilities as it is about the integrity of the surrounding landscapes and of the relationships between its operators, visitors, and the land. In this context history also plays a role, as it is important to honor the ancestral qualities of land and of the cultures that have been associated with it over time.

What is common for all of our clients in this field has been the need to expand the scope of their vision, and to include components of each other's programming: retreat centers now offer massage, shiatsu, and yoga; spas now invite visiting gurus and spiritual teachers. Add into this mix a wholehearted advocacy for sustainability and social responsibility, and the spa and retreat movement ranks among the more interesting social developments of recent times. Our clients in this area have included conventional spas in urban settings, retreat centers in remote areas, as well hybrids of these two trends. We have worked on spas in New York, Los Angeles, Hong Kong, Mexico, Jordan, and Japan, including Rancho La Puerta (Mexico), Golden Door (CA), Two Bunch Palms (CA), Mayflower Spa (MA), and Wadi Ram (Kingdom Jordan). Our contributions to retreat centers have included the Omega Institute (NY), Hollyhock (BC), Kripalu (MA), The Open Center (NY), and CoSM–The Chapel of Sacred Mirrors (NY).

Equinox Fitness
USA, Canada, and the UK

Equinox Group is an American fitness company headquartered in New York City, which operates several separate lifestyle brands: Equinox, Equinox Hotels, Precision Run, Project by Equinox, Equinox Explore, PURE Yoga, Blink Fitness, and SoulCycle. Equinox currently operates more than 300 fitness locations within major cities across the United States, as well as in London, Toronto, and Vancouver. In addition, the PURE Yoga brand operates yoga studios in the United States, Hong Kong, Shanghai, Singapore, and Taipei.

Equinox exemplifies a growing trend in the fitness industry which has increasingly incorporated alternative lifestyle components into its traditional fitness mix. Equinox was an early adopter of yoga and meditation and now offers metabolic and kinesiology testing for optimal health. It also pioneered a more sophisticated approach to the design and decor of the fitness space that incorporated advanced design, luxury decor, as well as feng shui and geomancy.

Fitness and Yoga

Once a separate business, fitness studios have increasingly incorporated aspects of wellness and health into their offerings. From yoga and meditation to zumba and crossfit, fitness gyms have rebranded themselves as lifestyle businesses intent on providing a wide suite of services embracing wellness and self-improvement. In the process, they have shedded their reputation for sweaty muscle-building in spartan basements to include remarkably elegant spaces, fashionable sportwear brands, and even nutrition and health advisory services. The addition of electronic aids, video streaming options, and app-based fitness tracking have ultimately helped produce brands that can now capture global markets. In the process, they have made significant contributions to the current trend for transformational experiences in the marketplace, although often with a generous tinge for self adulation and with a sometimes obvious reliance on celebrity endorsements.

In the mean time, yoga studios have made a transformation of their own, albeit in the opposite direction. What started in the 1970s as a spiritual search based on Eastern roots, today encompasses a global range of attitudes and offerings, many of which now focus on health and fitness in addition to the ever-present spirituality. In the process, they have also made their own contributions to the transformational nature of the consumer experience and brought into play brands that are now operating globally. This has provided the yoga audience with a dazzling array of choices–from the traditional neighborhood studio, to luxury brands of a truly global scale, including highly specialized boutique studios for niche audiences.

This two-way trend has had one important result: the creation of spaces with much higher architectural sophistication. Gone are by the most part the cavernous gyms replete with barbells or the grungy yoga studios featuring macrame and candles. Instead, both fitness and yoga establishments have enfolded top design talent to create environments that are both practical in terms of their programmatic requirements, as well as elegant and informed about aesthetics and evidence-based design. Feng shui has also been incorporated widely in both of these markets, partly as a bow to tradition in the case of yoga, but more and more as a way to create spaces resonant with vitality and dynamism, and also as a way to enhance opportunity for income generation, brand recognition, leadership, and customer loyalty. Our clients in these fields have included Pure Yoga, Mayflower Yoga, Rancho La Puerta, Golden Door, and Two Bunch Palms in the yoga realm as well as Equinox Fitness, Reebok Crossfit, and Montreal Mansfield Athletic in fitness.

CoSM
Chapel of Sacred Mirrors, Wappinger Falls, NY

The Chapel of Sacred Mirrors is a transdenominational church dedicated to the realization of a shared vision of the American artists Alex and Allyson Grey: to build a contemporary public chapel as a sanctuary for spiritual renewal through contemplation of transformative art. CoSM's stated mission is to "build an enduring sanctuary of visionary art to inspire every pilgrim's creative path and embody the values of love and evolutionary wisdom".

Currently located in a rural retreat center along the Hudson River, CoSM was conceived initially to house Alex Grey's *Sacred Mirrors*, a series of twenty-one art-works, which examine the body and its relationship to spirit and mind. CoSM is also an event space promoting lectures and spiritual teachings, which encourage an ecumenical approach to spirituality. Our contributions to CoSM included site selection, site planning, architectural design guidelines, rituals, and blessings for their retreat center in Wappinger Falls.

Spirituality & Healing

Creating sacred space is one of my top priorities, partly because feng shui and geomancy are ideally suited to this task, but also because landscapes are being de-sacralized at an alarming rate. Industry, urban sprawl, pollution, desecration through war and conflict, and the radicalization of ideology and religion are all threatening to destroy the web of sacredness that Nature and the Divine have placed at our disposal here on Earth. Recovering a respect for the holy, and allowing this to manifest with grace and natural beauty in the built environment, are contemporary challenges of unparalleled importance. In fact, it could be said this task supersedes all others, because without a sense of the sacred in everyday life, there is no possibility for conscious life, and therefore, no real possibility for sustainability in the long term. It is our responsibility as denizens of nature and as stewards of its beauty, power, and integrity, to make sure we can pass these qualities undisturbed and vibrant to the next generations.

Sacred spaces are alive, conscious, and inherently accessible to us. They interact with us and we interact with them, whether consciously or not. Sacred spaces afford humanity an opportunity to find ourselves again and again, to return to the personal and collective origins where we can discover our higher purpose. Because sacred spaces can only be created on hollowed ground, they hold a very special relationship with the earth and its manifestations in nature, the cosmos, and time. At their best, they can be used by humanity as a way to enhance our journey through life in a manner that elevates us and intensifies our relationships to divine, to the land, to self, and to others.

Our clients in this field have included organized religious groups, sacred artists, healers, hospitals, spas, and many individuals intent on creating a more sacred container for their lives, either through intentionally holy spaces, or through sacred areas in homes, offices, or gardens. Through active use, these sacred spaces become alive, and take on an identity not possible in other types of spaces or structures. The tools we have used for this purpose include classical feng shui, shamanic healing rituals, Indian Vastu design principles, sacred geometry, and European geomancy. Common to all of these is a deeply-seated respect for the sacredness of land and of space, and for the time continuum projected in our aspirations for health, happiness, and community.

Chalice Well and Healing Garden, Glastonbury, England

Chalice Well and its healing garden are among the most beloved spiritual places in all of Europe. Part of the pilgrimage route of Avalon and steeped in the Arthurian myths, Chalice Well has seen continuous spiritual activity since Neolithic times.

Located in the medieval town of Glastonbury, the well is part of the imposing complex that includes Glastonbury Tor, the Chalice Healing Garden, and the White Spring. The waters drawn from the well are renowned for their healing qualities and for their ability to awaken spiritual powers. The entire garden has been conceived as a journey into the self, with quiet areas for contemplation, outdoor meeting spaces, ablution ponds, and a public fountain for taking the waters.

Because this is one of my favorites places, I often come back to introduce students and pilgrims to its delights, and to study its hidden secrets. As with all healing gardens, I never tire of its magic, and always yearn to return.

Sacred Sites

Sacred sites provide critical learning experiences for geomancers. From our perspective, sacred sites are endowed with enormous power. From the very earliest times, humans have sought to identify locations that had special influences and ascribed to them numinous qualities akin to the divine. Mountains, springs, caves, venerable trees, rivers, and other features of the landscape have been clothed in meaning, symbolism, and magic. Every culture has done this, regardless of location, ethnicity, or cultural development. In some instances, as with the Huichol in Mexico, some cultures even venerate sacred sites far removed from their actual habitation, undertaking long pilgrimages to reach these far-flung places. Often, these connections across landscapes were used to create energy grids (*leys* or *seques*) that could be used to increase soil quality, enhance political power, and support sovereignty. Over time, these spiritual "girds" would grow to cover vast terrain.

Though all land is sacred, the fact is not all places are of equal power, nor do all sacred sites exhibit the same type of impact on humanity, flora, or fauna. Mountains tend to be imbued with masculine energy, whereas springs and wells partake of a more feminine quality. These distinctions can get very granular: certain rocks in Bretagne are renowed for their ability to promote fertility in women, but only at certain times; springs endowed with healing powers may be able to heal only one organ or part of the body; sacred rocks in Africa, Australia, and Amazonia are often places for discussion, inter-tribal conferencing, and political resolution; caves across the world are often places for deep healing and regeneration. The list goes on.

Sacred sites have also been used over millenia as places for sacred architecture. It used to be axiomatic that a sacred building could only be placed in land already sacred, but techniques were developed to connect land not sacred to land that was, allowing for construction of temples and healing architecture closer to urban centers. Unfortunately, today's religious architecture is often lacking in this basic understanding, with a resultant diminution of sacred qualities in religious practice around the world.

We have provided extensive guidance to clients and students interested in discovering, identifying, and measuring the power and sacredness of land. We also teach approaches to this power and to how to harness it for personal and collective use. This includes techniques for connecting homes, hospitals, gardens, and other spaces to sources of real power and sacredness in the land.

Space Clearing Ceremonies

Space clearing ceremonies are important components of every building project. Grounded in millenary traditional practices, Space Clearing rituals are both celebrations and initiations. They can be used to promote success, health, prosperity, and efficiency. They can also be used to address situations in which there has been misfortune, a loss, or health problems. Space clearings are particularly effective at opening up new opportunities to create more abundance in everyday life.

Space Clearing rituals have at their basis the restoration of energetic balance in an existing space or site. In most cases this involves an initial period of purification usually induced with incense or smoke, followed by a clearing of the softened energies by clapping or beating of drums, and then, a programming of the space to its intended uses by ringing of bells or other sound devices. Finally, a blessing is performed, usually involving prayer and meditational procedures proper to the tradition being used. The photo above shows shamanic blessing tools. At right, a Balinese space clearing offering.

Rituals and Ceremonies

Rituals and ceremonies are among the more interesting contributions of feng shui and geomancy to the building practices. They can be used to prepare the land for construction, to bless or consecrate buildings for a particular purpose, to clear out unwanted energies in existing buildings, and even to help with serious problems such as illness or misfortune. Site Blessings, for example, prepare the land for construction. Space Clearings are carried out before occupancy in new spaces. Sealing Rituals lock energies inside spaces in order to protect them and promote positive qualities. In all cases, rituals can be joyful events and are often accompanied by beautiful and lavish offerings. Many clients choose to open them up to their clients, friends, and the press, as they can make excellent public relations events.

Preparations for rituals can be extensive, and timing is often a significant factor. In general, rituals are keyed to the cycles of nature, the rotations of the sun and moon, the seasons, or other celestial events. Feng shui, in particular, has an array of tools, which are used to determine ideal times for ground-breaking ceremonies, initiation of construction, grand openings, signing of construction documents and leases, moving into new spaces, and so on. Use of these parameters provides a safe way to forestall any potentially negative consequences and to promote long-term success for the individuals or institutions involved.

Rituals and ceremonies can also be used to correct more serious problems such as geopathic stresses (negative energies in the land), unwanted legacies in existing buildings (negative predecessor energy), financial misfortune, poor health, bad neighborhood energy, and even ghosts and hauntings. Feng shui and its related variants in other traditions offer a wide variety of rituals that can be tailored to the specific circumstances encountered by the client. These include shamanic rituals, Vastu pujas, Shinto ceremonies, Balinese clearing rituals, Celtic house blessings, and many more. Some of the more common feng shui rituals include Yu Wei Rice Blessings, Realgar Sealing rituals, and Golden Cicada rituals for legal and conflict resolution. Shamanic rituals useful in construction include Despacho offerings that can be buried on site or burnt at the location, as well as Soul Retrievals to help heal ancestral wounds present in the land. Celtic Crystal rituals can be used to remediate geopathic stresses or to bless foundations. As this short list demonstrates, the wealth of rituals and ceremonies available is practically endless.

ALEX STARK is an internationally recognized consultant, advisor, and teacher on issues of creativity, efficiency, and design. A graduate of the Yale University School of Architecture, he is a practitioner of feng shui, oriental astrology, European geomancy, and Native American earth healing. He advises on issues of design and placement for residential, commercial, institutional, educational, and industrial facilities, urban settlements, health care facilities, and on issues of personal and institutional transformation.

Alex is a recipient of a Ford Foundation scholarship for cross-cultural studies and was named Scholar of the House by Yale University. He has worked for the United Nations Development Program in regional planning and public health. His clients include: Hyatt Corporation, Morgan Stanley, Conde Nast Publishing, Whole Foods Markets, Beth Israel Hospital, Bellevue Hospital, Continuum Center for Health & Healing, Sutter Health, Hyatt Retirement Residences, Prudential Douglas Elliman, Dean Witter, Blackstone Real Estate. Mack-Cali Realty, Reebok USA, Swarovski Crystals, David Yurman, The University of Minnesota, The Aspen Institute, The Four Seasons Hotels, One&Only Hotels, NBC Today Show, and many others.

Alex's work has been featured on NBC, CNN, PBS, the Arts & Entertainment Channel, *The New York Times, Town & Country, Crain's, Harper's, Inc., The Wall Street Journal, Interior Design, Residential Architecture, Interiors, Spirituality and Health, ID Magazine, Metropolis,* and others. He has received a design citation for his feng shui work by the Boston Society of Architects.

Alex has lectured at the Smithsonian Institution in Washington, Regents College in London, The University of Amsterdam, The University of California at Berkeley, the University of Minnesota Medical School, the University of Minnesota College of Architecture, the American Institute of Architects, the American Holistic Medical Association, the Symposium for Health Care Design, the International Academy for Design & Health, the Center for Health Design, the Feng Shui International Network in London, the European School of Feng Shui in Amsterdam, and the French School of Geomancy in Paris. He is a member of the faculty of the Omega Institute (NY), Hollyhock (Canada), the Long Island Feng Shui Institute (NY), the Golden Gate School of Feng Shui (CA), the Feng Shui Alliance (NJ), and the International Feng Shui School (Ireland).

ADRIANA STARK is Operations Manager for Alex Stark Feng Shui. She is in charge of client interphase, research, and architectural analysis for clients worldwide. In addition to her duties as Operations Manager, she is currently in charge of rituals and blessing for all of Europe and the UK. Adriana also brings to our firm her talents as an Interior Designer, with major interests in holistic design, adaptive reuse, sustainability, innovative materials, furniture design, and design as experience.

A native of New York City, Adriana holds an M.I.A. Degree from California State Polytechnic University of Pomona in Interior Architecture. She also holds an A.A. Degree from Bard College, a B.A. degree in Theater and Film Studies from Warwick University (UK), and an M.F.A. degree in Film Studies from University College London.

Adriana has trained in Compass School feng shui, BTB feng shui practice, and Native American cosmology. Her experience in the Arts have also served our firm by contributing to improved graphics, photography, and marketing materials. She has also worked as a professional photographer, having published three books of creative work.